PORTUGAL

BETWEEN EUROPE AND THE ATLANTIC

WHITE STAR PUBLISHERS

Text
Alberto Bertolazzi

Graphic design
Anna Galliani

Map
Cristina Franco

Contents

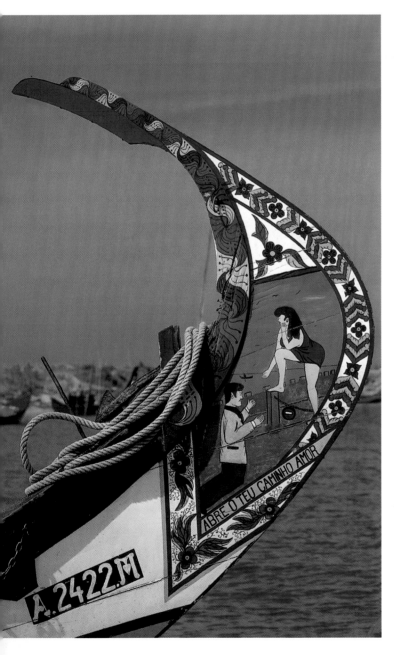

1 *The grand palace of Queluz is a rococo castle surrounded by French gardens near Lisbon: long used as a summer residence by the Portuguese ruling family, the Braganzas, it now houses a luxurious restaurant, the Cozinha Velha, patronized by Lisbon's VIPs.*

2-3 *Albufeira, is perhaps the most famous holiday resort on the Algarve coast, the ultimate seaside region in Portugal. Despite huge recent urban development, Albufeira has managed to conserve the characteristic Moorish style of the old fishing village.*

4-5 *All along the valley of the Rio Douro, the river that flows into the sea at Porto, the peasants have, over the centuries, laboriously dug thousands of terraces in the rock. They use these to grow one the most famous wine grapes in the world, the only true wealth of this region.*

6-7 *Ponta de Piedade displays the most stunning natural beauty offered by the Algarve: rocks with reddish-golden reflections rise from an emerald-green sea to form spectacular arches and deep inlets.*

8 *The moliceiros are characteristic boats of the south and were, in the past, used exclusively for fishing; now they are also built for the use of tourists. Some are painted simply in bright colors, others are masterpieces with their bows painted in naive style.*

9 *The Torre de Belém is a masterpiece of Portuguese Manueline style. Built on a rocky islet at the mouth of the Tagus estuary, the river that connects Lisbon with the Atlantic, the sea around the tower gradually silted up until it found itself in the immediate vicinity of the shore, where it is seen today.*

© 1998 White Star s.p.a.
Via C. Sassone, 22/24
13100 Vercelli, Italy
www.whitestar.it

New updated edition in 2007

ISBN 978-88-544- 0262-1

Reprints:
1 2 3 4 5 6 11 10 09 08 07

Color separation by Graphic Service, Milan and CTM, Turin

Printed in Italy

10 top left *The obstinate nature of the Portuguese people is shown by signs left on the land: every tiny patch of arable territory has been terraced, even on distant islands. The picture shows Pico, in the Azores.*

10 top right *Estremoz, in the Alentejo, was a royal residence during the golden era. The castle where Vasco da Gama received gifts to take to the Indies is now a pousada, or hotel, and has preserved its "period" settings and atmosphere to perfection.*

10 center left *Obidos survived the forays that despoiled the Costa da Prata over the centuries thanks to its position (raised and inland) and to solid walls that still run all round it today.*

10 center right *Coimbra is considered the "third capital" of Portugal, after Lisbon and Porto. Its role in culture and research, its world-famous university, and its lively atmosphere make it one of the driving forces of Portuguese development.*

10 bottom *The Claustro Real, at Batalha, is universally accepted as a masterpiece of Manueline style. In fact, the cloister, like the rest of the monastery, is a blend of various styles, with a predominance of Gothic and Manueline.*

12-13 *The Portuguese have always had to deal with the sea. The birth, development, and decline of imperial Portugal were the direct result of the close relationship between country and ocean. This is evident all along the coast where entire communities still make a living from fishing.*

14-15 *Terceira is one of the nine islands of the archipelago of the Azores. Together with Madeira, it is all that remains of Portuguese dominions overseas.*

16-17 *The Baixa, literally "lower town," is one of the most elegant districts in Lisbon. Its "French" plan is the fruit of the reconstruction following the 1755 earthquake.*

ATLANTIC
OCEAN

SPAIN

VIANA DO
CASTELO

Rio Lima

BRAGA

Rio Cavado

BRAGANZA

Rio Tamega

VILA REAL

Costa Verde

PORTO

ESPINHO

Rio Douro

Rio Douro

Serra de Mogadouro

M O U N T A I N S

Costa da Prata

FIGUEIRA

COIMBRA

Rio Mondego

*Serra da
Estrela*

NAZARÉ

BATALHA

FATIMA

TOMAR

OBIDOS

SANTARÉM

PORTALEGRE

River Tagos

E S T R E M A D U R A

SINTRA

Rio Sorraia

CABO DA ROCA

LISBON

ESTREMOZ

CASCAIS

*Mar da
Palha*

ESTORIL

EVORA

SETUBAL

*Bay of
Setubal*

Rio Sado

A L E N T E J O

Costa Dourada

Rio Guadiana

BEJA

Rio Mira

A L G A R V E

CABO DE SÃO VICENTE

LAGOS

ALBUFEIRA

TAVIRA

FARO

SAGRES

*Bay of
Lagos*

*Gulf of
Cadiz*

Introduction

On that mild winter's day, his gaze swept over the cultivated Alentejo plain, the land lying "across the river Tagus." All the shades of green were there, and a crisp breeze blew from Spain. That day Dom Manuel would speak to him of a journey that would change the future of Portugal. Vasco da Gama was not yet thirty but he was the leading figure in the school of navigation conceived and run by Henry the Navigator. Henry was a great monarch, of the kind that make history. Despite his nickname he had never ventured farther than Morocco, yet he understood the sea. In his villa at Sagres – built more or less on what the ancients believed was the edge of the world – he had met the best sailors, studied the winds, the known seas and lands, and he had realized that the only way to go was towards the high seas. The art of navigation spoke Portuguese; they had been fishermen since time immemorial, relegated to a narrow strip of land and restricted by a cumbersome neighbor; in that period of the fifteenth century, the Portuguese were hemmed in.

The fields, those viewed absently-mindedly by Vasco da Gama from the Estremoz Fortress, were no longer sufficient. The peasants were starving, the fieldoms were repeatedly shaken by revolts, and rumours were spreading from the port towns that somewhere on the other side of the ocean immense riches were waiting to be loaded into ship holds.

It was true that, so far, the great expeditions organized by Henry the Navigator and João II had brought neither gold nor diamonds -- just a few islands in the Atlantic (the Azores, Madeira, and the Capo Verde islands), a tangle of forests where the air seethed with insects (the Congo), and a headland at the tip of Africa around which the sea raged like the inferno. There, at the Cape of Storms, sighted ten years earlier by Bartholomeu Diaz, the young Vasco was to take wing. In May 1498, after fourteen months of navigation and having rounded what he had renamed the Cape of Good Hope, da Gama landed in Calicut. The route to India was open and with it the rich trade between Europe and Asia was transferred from crowded and dangerous land routes to the immense oceanic motorway. From that moment nothing would be inconceivable, nothing would be forbidden. In 1500, Brazil, the most precious -- and remunerative -- of the jewels on the crown, was "discovered" and colonized.

The adventure of great expeditions that started in the heart of the flat, rural Alentejo plain – where then and still now the peasants' faces, like the furrows of the land, seem change – altered the geography and distribution of power on earth. From that moment and for nearly three hundred years, Portugal ranked as a Great Power. Its empire extended to the five continents: from Brazil to Macao, ships were sailing loaded with slaves and returning laden with gold. Its bothersome neighbor – the great Spain – was forced to capitulate and call for the signing of the treaty of Tordesillas (a forerunner of Yalta), which sanctioned the "bloodless" division of the New World.

The Alentejo and the colonies, rural Portugal and the promised lands, poverty and wealth: all Portuguese history passed through Estremoz on that memorable day in 1497, as if through a huge eye of a needle. This was the beginning of the greatness and the poverty of present-day Portugal, a country striving to live for the future, gambling on Europe, tourism, and technology, but never ceasing to mourn a colossal, extraordinary past.

Estremoz and the Alentejo, the granary of Portugal, as it has always been considered, is actually the home of cork. The outstanding quality of the alentejano oak bark has resulted in record exports to wine-producing countries (the area supplies two-thirds of all the corks made in the world). However, the poverty is manifest: the few cars on the roads are either driven by foreigners or are out-of-date models, the roads are as dusty as paths, the houses seem uninhabited, and the shop windows reflect the people's reluctance to spend. Economic development has not visited these narrow country roads nor the brightly-lit, far from crowded, rural villages.

Equally manifest, however, is the inner wealth of the inhabitants. The Dukes of Braganza, who were Portugal's last monarchs, lived here and this shows more in the proud and noble spirit of the people than in the castles and the ancient convents, often now turned into *pousadas*, (hotels). In this land, just a few miles from the industrialized belt that runs from Lisbon, via Setúbal, to Santarém, footsteps are slow, the eyes gentle and mournful, the faces tanned and worn, and the hands large and hardened.

The landscape, unchanged since the times of Vasco da Gama, has brought this region the name of *planicies*, or "plains," dotted with fields cultivated mainly with wheat, cork plantations, and olive groves, a cluster of white houses at the foot of a castle, flocks of sheep and herds of pigs, the odd bull. Not even tourism has enriched the Alentejo. Only the pick of travelers come here, those who want to retreat into the *pousadas*, to relive the aristocratic atmosphere of good times past, or to breathe what remains of that revolutionary spirit that made this a pre-eminently "red" region.

It is at Vila Viçosa and Évora that the Alentejo conserves the most spirited images of its contradictory past. Vila Viçosa was a residence of the Braganza family, the last dynasty to have ruled in Portugal. Their end, which came about *de facto* in 1908 with the assassination of King Carlos I and the Crown Prince, coincided with a definitive reawakening from dreams of glory and the start of the nation's modern history, one of dictatorship and democracy, poverty and rebirth. The splendid ducal palace of Vila Viçosa, with its dimly-lit rooms and cool orange-groves, is a melancholic keepsake of monarchical Portugal, abandoned in the center of a square renamed, ironically, Praça da Republica. Évora is still enclosed within its Manueline walls. Its urban design and the sixteenth-century university have come through centuries of decline

18 top Tavira is an attractive town situated just over 12 miles from the border with Spain, on the Algarve coast. Paradoxically, it owes part of its success with holidaymakers to the 1755 earthquake which produced marine movements that silted up part of the port. Bathers now flock to those beaches.

18 bottom Tavira is divided in two by the Rio Asséca. A well-preserved seventeenth-century bridge connects the two quarters, one of which is dominated by the ruins of a Moorish castle.

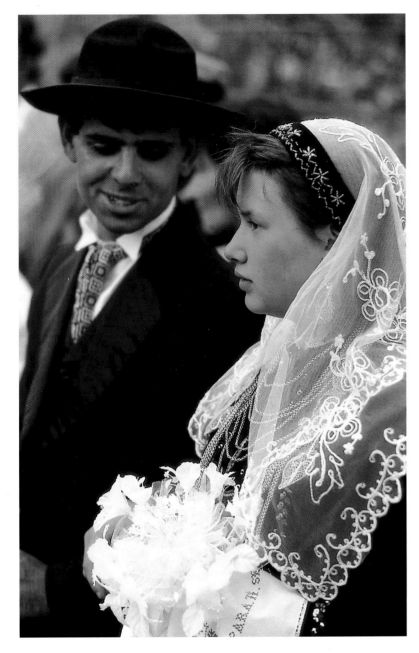

without a blemish. Only the church of São Francisco and the nearby Capela dos Ossos suggest the by no means quick nor light passage of time. A hanged skeleton serves as the backdrop to this famous chapel of meditation the walls lined with human skulls and bones. An inscription warns, the bones resting here are awaiting yours."

The Alentejo is a kaleidoscope of delightful visions. It is features a thousand colors, as in the wool carpets made at Arraiolos, a village of white houses known the world over for its products of mediaeval origin and flavor. It is mysterious, as demonstrated by the ninety-five *menhirs* abandoned in protohistoric times in the middle of a forest of cork oaks at Almendres. It can be virulent, like the *Alentejan* bulls. More fortunate than their Spanish brothers, they do not risk their lives during bullfights: no bulls have been slaughtered in the Portuguese bullrings since Duke d'Arcos was killed during a *tourada*, and their horns are sheathed. Actually should they suffer injury they are nursed to a full recovery. The Alentejo is the underdeveloped hinterland of Lisbon, the warped reflection of the history, ambitions, and decadence of the capital. Trás-os-Montes, Beira Alta, and the Douro Valley regions conventionally defined as *montanhas* are the same for Porto, the secondmost densely populated and important town in Portugal.

The barren plains of the centraleast conserve the seeds of that haughty desire for adventure that made Lisbon great, but the mountains of the north have produced the tenacity and fighting spirit of the most industrial Portuguese cities. "Tenacious" is the only way to describe the fight for survival of the peoples living in Trás-os-Montes, an arid region where icy winds blow for six months of the year and that nevertheless conserves small, ancient communities that live on tradition and stockbreeding. "Enterprising" is the only possible definition of the spirit of those farmers that in historical times already worked the hills of the Rio Douro ("river of gold") valley in to terraces, creating, despite droughts and with huge efforts, vineyards renowned all over the world. Again, wealth and poverty come and go in these regions far from the sea. On the one hand, the men have an unmatched dignity and pride, the towns bear extraordinary marks of history, and the landscapes glow with a rare and sanguine beauty. On the other hand, the land offers a difficult climate, a hard everyday life, unprofitable crops, and backward social customs.

Symbolic of the beauty and harshness of these lands, featuring an alternation of vineyards, semi-desert areas, and woodsof chestnut and pine, the splendid city of Braganza is set on a hill in the extreme northeast of the country. Its citadel is a masterpiece of mediaeval architecture and has survived perfectly intact to this day. Its circle of walls, which can be followed all the way around along the walkways, its well-preserved urban plan, the Managem Tower, and the cathedral are the jewels of a unique and little-known village. More famous are Castelo Branco and Vila Real: the former conserves the remains of fortifications, a reminder of the constant contacts between these regions and Spanish invaders, and first-class examples of Portuguese baroque style (above all, the Jardim Episcopal, the loveliest gardens

19 *In Viana do Castelo, a lovely little town north of Porto just a few miles from Spain, the famous Romaria da Senhora da Agonia, the best-known religious festival held in northern Portugal is held in August. For three days, pilgrims from all over the country are entertained by fireworks, bull races, and costume parades.*

20-21 *Madeira, the largest island of the archipelago of the same name, was defined "part of the world but beyond the world" by Luis de Camões. Of extreme beauty but lying out in the middle of the ocean, it has played host to princes and aristocrats, on holiday or exiled, as well as generations of permanent residents who owe their survival to a little farming and much fishing.*

in the country); Vila Real, besides for automobile races, is known for the Mateus *solar*, an estate belonging to the counts of Vila Real, who produce the famous wine exported all over the world.

Wine is the most obvious heritage that the Douro has passed on to Porto, the city near the mouth of the "river of gold." The good quality wine, inexpensive and drunk young, such as the *vinho verde* (green wine), or mellowed, such as port, is appreciated everywhere and exported to all parts of the world. *Vinho verde* owes its name to the fact that the grapes used to make it are harvested when still partially unripe. It is produced all over the Douro Valley, drunk cool, and has a low alcohol content. Porto is not just a wine, it is the exemplification of the full-bodied and rich soul of the Portuguese people. High in alcoholic content, made with a variety of blends, and *ad hoc* ageing make it versatile and multiform. It can be drunk as an aperitif, a table wine (accompanying humble foods such as cornmeal bread, cheese and olives, or characteristic Arab-Portuguese desserts such as *papos de anjo* or *touchinho do ceu*, with honey, almonds, figs, and cinnamon), or when relaxing. It will warm stomach and heart, revive conversation, or accompany the wistful melody of the *fado*. The port-producing vineyards also symbolize how the Portuguese see themselves: short and sturdy, clinging to the schistose slopes of the valley, they push their roots deep into the ground to withstand the fury of events and draw up the few resources that a mean land is loath to let go. No storms, snow, gusts of wind, or drought will shake these vines. They have always produced tasty grapes, which in some *quintas* (wine-estates with cellars) are still pressed by foot.

The history of *vinho do Porto* embraces much of the history of Portugal, starting in 1642 when, after a century of wars at sea, a peace treaty with England opened the way for trade between the two countries. Port was officially born in those years, apparently invented in 1668 by two English importers who came up with the idea of adding spirits to stabilize it for the long journey. Much progress has been made since then, yet just thirty years ago the wine was still being transferred from the *quintas* to Porto on *barcos rabelos*, sailing craft of Visigoth origin that guaranteed slow movement and few jolts. Portugal is an incredible country: nearly everywhere in the Western world, manual labor has been replaced by chips and gears but in the Douro Valley, during the grape harvest, men still carry funnel-shaped baskets laden with 150 pounds of grapes on their shoulders up and down the winding hills. This toil is rewarded with little money and much glory. Portuguese wine travels all over the world, but not before it has rested in oak vats for at least three years. The best is aged in bottles, sometimes for forty years, to produce late vintages that are second to none.

Porto, the final stop in wine production, is the capital of the Costa Verde, a splendid region dominated by sea and history, as well as a devotion to work. "Coimbra sings, Braga prays, Lisbon plays politics, and Porto works." This old saying is repeated with some

satisfaction in the capital of the north, the leading business and secondmost important industrial center in the country. With its ocean fog and Nordic-like levels of rainfall, this is where the most European Portugal is to be seen, rattling across the Dom Luis I Bridge over the Douro River, or slipping from the vineyards of Gondomar into the hard heart of the city – the port of Leixões. Eyes that gaze at the ocean here are not filled with nostalgia: they look towards Europe.

Porto is not really beautiful, but it is intriguing. Although grey and foggy for most of the year, it is luminous as only an ocean city can be. Full of parks, it blossoms in spring like a Mediterranean metropolis, smelling of grapes and salt. Just one true "seamen's" district remains: Ribeira. In this tangle of narrow streets, the houses look onto one another, damp and, for the most part, crumbling, yet quaint and rather alarming because they have not yet been abandoned, indeed they are very much alive. The shops, as noisy as Oriental markets, the smells, bitter and subtle as befits a seafaring village, and the poor people, who have not yet been evicted from the houses of an old city center that attracts no building speculators, are as a common sight as in Genoa, Naples, Palermo, Barcelona, Marseilles, Athens, and Lisbon too: all great seafaring cities that do not disown their history, bound to fishing and hence to hunger.

However, the history of Porto is also one of industry and trade, and therefore wealth. This is visible in its baroque churches: from that of São Francisco, with its typically opulent gilded carvings made in 1753 using nearly 500 pounds of gold from the Brazilian colony, to the Igreja dos Clerigos, built at the height of the city's splendor in the eighteenth century, on an oval plan and with the highest belltower in Portugal (the Torre dos Clerigos, 250 feet high with 225 steps).

The new wealth can be perceived in the shops that line the streets of the old center, where the medieval tradition of streets "specializing" in just one trade. This habit of specialization can also be seen in some of the local restaurants, including those serving *dobrada a moda do Porto* (simply veal tripe, chicken, and beans), which is not a humble dish, but a regional gastronomic masterpiece. With a touch of snobbery perhaps, the city's VIPs will meet at the *O Tripeiro* (tripe restaurant) rather than *O Escondidinho* and prefer what used to be the food of the poor to the squid, oysters, salmon, and lobster regularly served at popular restaurants.

A taste of well-being can also be had along the Miramar beach or at Espinho, with its modern luxury hotels and numerous golf clubs, or a few miles farther north at the ocean port of Viana do Castelo; here busy shipyards, a fishing fleet, aristocratic villas dating from the late-Manueline period, a square – Praça da Republica – of rare beauty, and the original iron-bridge designed by Eiffel give the visitor the impression of something more than an elegant seaside resort. The Costa Verde is also a treasure chest of natural wealth become, in recent years, a tourist attraction. The countryside, green as the name of the region suggests, benefits from plentiful rainfall and presents a charming alternation of hills and plains,

22 top Every year more than a million pilgrims come from all over the world to visit the sanctuary of Fátima. The pilgrimage season starts officially in the middle of May and ends around mid-October. By tradition, the first and last pilgrimages are the most crowded.

22 bottom The Alentejo ("the land across the river Tagus") is considered the granary of Portugal. Actually it is, above all, the region of corks. The cultivation of cork oaks has made this region the world's leading cork exporter. More than two-thirds of all wine corks purchased on the five continents originate here.

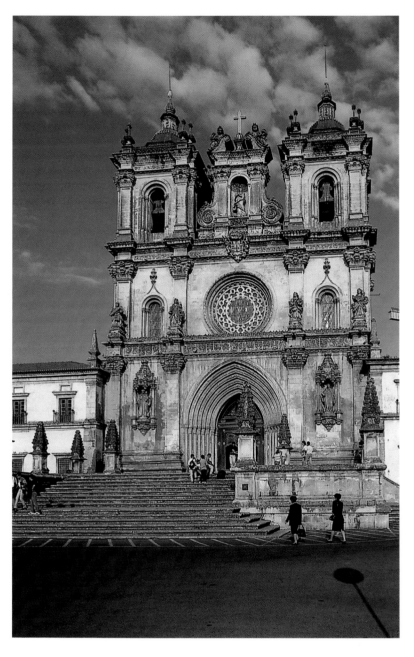

23 *On the main square of Alcobaça, a little town inland of the Costa da Prata, famous for its wines and liqueurs, stands the splendid Abbey of Santa Maria, a monastery founded by the Cistercians in the middle of the twelfth century. Interesting tours can be taken of to the huge kitchens, the so-called "cloister of silence," and the tombs of Pedro I and Inés de Castro.*

24-25 *The University of Coimbra is the most important in the country and one of the most famous in the world. Its library is a fine example of early eighteenth-century baroque architecture. The ceilings feature much tromp l'oeil decoration, a technique borrowed from the great French mansions and applied here with the use of rich materials (gold, wood, marble) and stucco-work. Most of the decorations are inspired by the exploits of imperial Portugal, with references to the colonial dominions on the five continents. The immense library archives also conserve precious mediaeval works.*

chestnut woods and open valleys, dotted with vineyards small country houses in granite. The coast is still intact, lined with beaches of fine sand, on which the seaside amenities are often hidden – as at Praia do Ofir – between the ocean-side dunes and pine-tree woods.

The sea does not only represent Portugal's past. Beaches of fine Atlantic sand are scattered along the Costa de Prata, descending towards Lisbon, and characterize the south of the country. Inland, along the road between the two "capitals," that of the north and that of the south, is the third, Coimbra. Once the administrative capital, today it is a capital of culture – because of its ancient university – and of the *fado*. Beautiful and elegant as at Nazaré, with its fishermen and splendid unadulterated beaches a world-famous and timeless image, the Costa da Prata is not a "riviera" in the seaside sense of the word. It does not resemble the Algarve, land of tourism, warm Mediterranean winds, and lush vegetation. It is rather the epitome of coastal Portugal: harsh and gentle, refined and common, battered by the ocean winds in winter and a tropical sun in summer. The beaches, some refined such as those of Estoril and Cascais, two of the most famous resorts on the south coast, are crowded nonetheless. Estoril, renowned for its famous casino and sumptuous villas hidden by greenery, is perhaps the most elegant seaside resort. Cascais, although no longer a fishing village, conserves the traits of a small seafaring village with low, brightly-colored houses, narrow streets, and bars and restaurants along the sea shore. High-class houses and gardens have brought prestige to Benfica, one of the capital's old suburbs, famous for the Palácio do Marques de Fronteira, a lovely seventeenth-century villa with two splendid period gardens, and for the huge stadium that hosts the exploits of Lisbon's leading soccer team, one of the most celebrated in Europe. Pomp and splendor also shine at Queluz, in the summer residence of the royal household, the "Versailles of Portugal", and at Sintra, which possesses the country's most extraordinary castle, the Castelo da Pena. Remarkable and impressive is the section of the Aqueduto das Aguas Livres that crosses the Alcantara valley. It took more than three hundred years to complete and thus resolve the capital's eternal problem: drought.

From the small towns to Lisbon is no short leap. Although the countryside and seafaring villages have provided the Portuguese capital with manpower since the Middle Ages, Lisbon is today a cosmopolitan city, overcrowded and bewildering, where the pace is fast and every minute counts. Lisbon is a city of a thousand faces: the westernmost European capital, it is firmly anchored to the continent but always turned to the Atlantic. Its survival was long bound to its two seas: the Mar de Palha, "Sea of Straw," formed by the wide mouth of the Tagus River, and the Atlantic Ocean, sailed by caravels and galleons, fishing boats and whalers. Lisbon conserves the fascination of what was once the maritime capital of the post-Renaissance world: the *ruas*, narrow alleyways common to seafaring towns, the low, brightly-lit, colorful houses of Alfama or Belém, the fragrant and mercantile Arab-style squares that give way to and the wide *avenidas*, the eighteenth-century

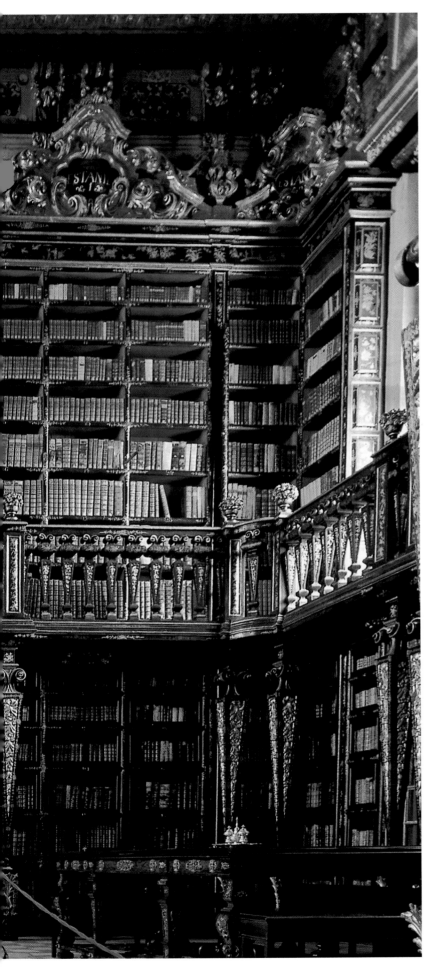

palaces of the Baixa, and the immense gardens that surround the loveliest *praças* (squares).

The charm of Lisbon also lies in the beauty of the bay in front of it, in the Atlantic mists, and the fresh water of the Tagus River that originates in Spain and flows into the ocean from a strange bulb-shaped mouth. On the vast northern shores of this lagoon (called "Sea of Straw" for its golden reflections), amid hills sloping from the Estremadura and the waters of the Tagus, is the loveliest part of Lisbon. Crossed on the *electricos*, the picturesque trams that trudge up and down its streets, seen from the *elevador*, unusual lifts that link the lower and upper cities, or admired from the ferries that connect it to the southern shore, the historic center of the capital is both luminous and intriguing, sweet and solemn. The view from the castle of São Jorge down onto the Praça do Comércio, the colored houses, the gardens of Belém and as far as the interminable Ponte 25 Abril (April 25th Bridge) brings an old Portuguese proverb to mind that says "*Quem nao tem visto Lisboa, nao tem visto cousa boa*" (He who has not seen Lisbon, has never seen beauty).

For its historical ups and downs and for the melting pot of cultures it has hosted, Lisbon is many cities in one. Every district possesses a sort of biological impression: the Bairro Alto and Alfama preserve traces of the Muslim presence and present the most cheerful and boisterous signs of everyday life; the Baixa, Rossio, Chiado, and the Praça do Comércio, fashioned by the aristocratic and wealthy hand of ancient Portuguese nobility, reflect the elegance of good times past. Diversity is one of its most obvious traits and is best summarized by the Manueline style, a mixture of the most varied artistic forms, of sea, epic, sacred, and profane motifs, all held together by a proud and daring love of conquest and discovery.

The inhabitants of Lisbon remember with great bitterness the event which, in their minds, changed the history of the city and that of all Portugal. On All Saint's Day 1755, an earthquake razed much of the city to the ground and a sixth of the population was buried under the ruins. Until that moment, the glory of Lisbon and that of Portugal had been one: as Paris for France or London for England, the city represented the whole nation. It was a long journey, from the Phoenicians, who had founded it as *Alis Ubbo* ("sweet bay") to the Arabs, who renamed it *al-Aschbouna* and contributed towards its Eastern appearance, clearly visible in all the districts bearing an Arab name (Alfama, Alcantara, Mouraria), to the mythical gold era sung by the poet Luís Camões and immortalized in inimitable monuments. But the decline of the maritime empires was just around the corner: the calamity that struck in the middle of the eighteenth century may have wounded the Portuguese soul and changed the civil structure of Lisbon more than it actually affected the history of Portugal. It was a historic coincidence of strong symbolical rather than practical value. The reconstruction, costly and hasty, guided by the Portuguese Richelieu, the Marques de Pombal, showed that it was not the public coffers that were spent in that ruinous eighteenth century, but the colonial experience, and with it the survival of those maritime powers that had failed to create an economic structure that would integrate the exploitation of overseas possessions in the homeland. Portugal was not England, which imported from its colonies the raw materials that fueled the Industrial Revolution. The country, in the late 1700s, was falling behind the times and missing the opportunity for new wealth.

Since decline of the Portuguese empire, only the magnificent beauty of the squares built by Pombal and the completely rebuilt Baixa district remains. Nothing has changed in the Portuguese capital since the time of that huge urban renovation, save for the recent economic boom and its symbols, the skyscrapers, shopping centers, and the Expo '98 pavilions. The oldest Lisbon, a port-city of a clearly Arab imprint, no longer really exists. Substantial traces have been preserved, especially in the Alfama, the old district of the Moors and prostitutes, a tangle of streets and alleys, washing hung out between one house and another, and tiny squares. Having survived the earthquake, thanks perhaps to the thermal system that serves as a foundation to its houses and which probably gave it its name (*al-Hama*, or baths), Alfama lies on the slope that descends from São Jorge towards the Tagus. In the Middle Ages, the notables of Lisbon lived there; later it became a residential quarter, first Arab and Jewish, then of fishermen and tradesmen. In the times of Pombal it had become a "ghetto" of prostitutes and sailors, a breeding ground for disease that Pombal, himself would have razed to the ground. Today, this lost opportunity for improvement works for the tourist industry. Cleansed of its bacteria, Alfama retains the strong fragrances and cries of the people from the small shops that open onto the alleys, large pots of rubber plants at the corners of the squares, ancient fountains (such as the Chafariz d'el Rei), the oldest church in Lisbon (Sé Patriarcal), the most unusual private building (Casa dos Bicos, with a diamond-pointed stone façade), and the most genuine spirit of the people embodied in the Feira da Ladra, the flea market of Campo de Santa Clara, where shoppers, though often swindled, can find excellent bargains.

The other three cardinal points of Lisbon are Praça do Comércio, the Rossio, and the Baixa. Praça do Comércio, or Terreiro do Praço, is practically a terrace with a small flight of steps extending towards the Tagus and affording views of the Atlantic. It is one of the loveliest squares in Europe, according to those who have visited it over the centuries, from Byron to Mann. The Rossio, officially the Praça de Dom Pedro IV, is airy and vibrant: it is the setting for the *movida* (night-life) of Lisbon, partly thanks to the Teatro Nacional Dona Maria II, one of the hubs of society life.

The Baixa, the lower town destroyed by the earthquake, was redesigned by Pombal according to the architectural standards in vogue just after the middle of the eighteenth century prescribing straight wide roads and elegant "Parisian-style" mansions.

This is the most European district of Lisbon: the shops on the main thoroughfares (Rua Aurea, Rua Augusta, Rua da Prata) are some of the most exclusive in the city; the houses in the Baixa are the most sought-after and consequently the most expensive.

Other parts of the city conserve the memory of old Lisbon. The Bairro Alto, the ancient "journalists' quarter," and dominates the city from the top of a hill is linked to the Baixa by an unusual lift (Elevador do Carmo). The elegant and unfortunate Chiado, long a point of reference for the society and cultural life of Lisbon, was greatly damaged by fire in 1988. Belém is home to the Tower of Belém and the Manueline Mosteiro dos Jerónimos – two of the most beautiful and prestigious buildings of Portuguese artistic history –, and the brightly-colored, narrow seventeenth-century houses of Rua Vieira Portuense. The castle of São Jorge, which closes the city to the rear, is more a park and scenic spot than a fortress.

Lisbon is rich in history and art and is wellequipped to its heritage. It boasts the Museu Nacional de Arte Antiga, filled with records, some critical, of colonial imperialism (as is the case of the Japanese *namban*, which tell of the cruelty that accompanied the Portuguese conquests as seen through the eyes of those being colonized), to the Museu d'Agua Manuel de Maia (which records the difficult struggle against the problem of water shortage in the Portuguese capital), the Museu Nacional dos Coches, displaying some of the loveliest carriages of European aristocratic history, the Museu Nacional do Teatro, the Museu Nacional do Azulejo, and the Museu da Marioneta. Unusual and disquieting, the Museu Arqueologico was set up in the ruins of the Igreja do Carmo. The church, built in the fourteenth century, is a ghostly reminder of the earthquake. Its Gothic arcades, some of the few medieval parts that survived the tremor, support no vaults, and concerts are held among its roofless aisles in summer. It was never reconstructed because Lisbon wanted to remember that terrible day with an unconventional monument: nothing could be better suited than these gutted ruins.

Not all is historical in Lisbon, but all is history. The capital has been, and wants to remain, the point of reference of that part of Portugal that still believes in great undertakings, as is demonstrated by three works completed this century. The Padrão dos Descobrimentos was commissioned in the years of the Salazar dictatorship, perhaps to boost its popularity. Today, with its row of heroes sculpted on the bow of a ship on the Tagus River, from Henry the Navigator to Vasco da Gama, it is an indication of the genuine bond between the peripheral post-colonial metropolis to that of the empire. The Padrão rises opposite the majestic statue of Cristo Rei and the 25 Abril Bridge, the longest suspension bridge on the old continent. These were also strongly desired by Salazar. After the dictator's fall, they became a symbol of rebirth: the former, with its great significance for humanity, links Lisbon ideologically to Rio de Janeiro, the other Portuguese-speaking city to have its landscape dominated by Christ the Redeemer (and with which Portugal maintains excellent business relations); the latter, reminiscent of the San Francisco Golden Gate, connects Lisbon with the south of the country, but, most of all, lends a concrete form to the solid and proud spirit of the Portuguese people, dreamers capable of great works.

Every building of note, every flight of steps, every fountain and tower built after the sixteenth century bears the sometimes overbearing mark of the *azulejos*, omnipresent tiles peculiar to Portugal, as are Manueline style and the *fado*. In the noble dwellings of the seventeenth century, the *azulejos* took the form of *tapetes* ("tapestries") covering whole walls. In the eighteenth-century churches, the massive late-baroque decorations are flanked by large panels depicting the lives

27 Azulejos, *an extraordinary
example of unconventional art, are
ceramic tiles painted to changing
canons, styles, and subjects, kiln-fired,
and widely applied in Portugal for
decorative requirements. Some churches
(such as the church of São Ildefonso in
Porto, shown here) exhibit* tapetes
("tapestries") of azulejos *on religious
themes instead of the traditional
frescoes. The history of the* azulejos
*reflects that of the country. Imported
by the Arabs during their stay on
Portuguese soil, they have over the
centuries reflected in turn Italian,
Flemish, and even Afro-American
tastes and manufacturing methods.
The decorations and the use of color
are an indication of the culture that
inspired them: blue and white with
stylized and mainly geometrical designs
were produced during the Moorish
domination (the Koran prohibited the
representation of human figures);
polychrome and depicting courtly scenes
– from hunting to love scenes – were
made at times of major trading
relations with northern Europe; religious
subjects prevailed during the years of
the Counter-Reformation; and themes
bound to seafaring conquests appeared
at the height of colonialism.*

28-29 *The monastery of Santa Maria da Vitória is a successful blend of Manueline, Renaissance, and Gothic styles. Its construction was started in 1385 at Batalha to celebrate the victory of the Portuguese over the Spanish at the battle of Aljubarrota. The sober and refined complex took over two hundred years to complete and boasts fine decorations in the ogives and along the portal. Of great beauty is the Claustro Real, or "royal cloister."*

30-31 *The internal courtyard of Mosteiro dos Jerónimos, in Lisbon, is perhaps the best-known example of Manueline style in Portugal. The wealth of decoration, mainly based on marine themes (a hawser motif is repeated along the entire length of the immense building), the precious materials, and the majesty of the complex make the Mosteiro one of the major works of art in the country.*

32-33 *Praça Dom Pedro IV, known to the citizens of the capital as "the Rossio," is one of the cardinal points of Lisbon. Circular in shape, embellished with large fountains, surrounded by historical buildings of great value (including the unmistakable profile of the Teatro Nacional Dona Maria II, seen in the background), and featuring numerous restaurants and bars, it is the point where the main city thoroughfares meet and is the hub of the Lisbon* movida.

of the saints painted on ceramics. At street corners, even in the less elegant districts, votive illustrations and street numbers are painted on brightly-colored tiles. As for nearly all aspects of Portuguese life, the *azulejos* are the fruit of a coming together of different cultures, from the simple blue-white tiles of Arab origin to the more complex and colored ceramics of Italian or Flemish inspiration, from the geometrical Eastern-style decorations to religious or aristocratic subjects.

The reflection of long centuries of Portuguese history, *azulejos* are more common on the coast, especially in Lisbon, than inland. The reason is clear: the sea ports experienced ethnic influxes of all types, from the Arab invasions to the "rebound" migrations from the colonies. Here the different flairs, a bit African, a bit Latin-American, a bit European, are concentrated and blend to raise these ceramic squares from mere tiles to works of art. And it is here, on the Atlantic coast but above all in the capital, that the ethnic differences produce the most unusual cultural and racial mixes: dark skin and green eyes, African bodies and Mediterranean features.

Portugal has a thousand faces but just one soul. For those not born within the narrow Portuguese boundaries, its soul may be the melody heard in the small bars, in Lisbon as in Coimbra too, sung by a *fadista* and played on two guitars. This is the *fado*, popular Portuguese music, a melancholic song perhaps taken from the troubadours of Provence, perhaps from Brazil or Africa: a cultural undertow, another rebound of the colonial heritage, that materializes to great effect in the *saudade*, impossible to translate but which means more or less "indulge languidly in nostalgia." This mood is peculiar to the Portuguese, even the most dynamic.

Portugal is a strange country, a land of bold enterprise and passive abandonment, of monotony and originality, of wealth and poverty, but never ordinary, not even in the most "touristy" areas such as the Algarve, a coast of rare beauty with a flattering and well-deserved name (*al-Gharb*, in Arabic "garden of the west"). This area is an Afro-Mediterranean garden where olive groves and orange and lemon trees stand alongside carob, almond, and fig tree. The climate, warm and temperate thanks to the mountains protecting the Algarve from the cold winds of the north, has made it a bathers' paradise. The coasts, flat and sandy to the west, rugged and broken by tiny beaches farther south, are the new promised land for hundreds of thousands of tourists seeking an untamed territory. A little building speculation, inevitable wherever there is money – especially if foreign –, has not yet changed the face of the region that housed the general headquarters of Henry the Navigator.

Some swear that the next new challenge to the world will start from Portugal, as in the fifteenth century, but not on galleons and caravels. The heroes of the year 2000 will control bathing establishments, museums, and tourist itineraries. From conquerors to conquered, the Portuguese will find gold and riches at home, by promoting and exploiting, at last, the exceptional natural and historical riches of a land that was once stretched to the ends of the world.

Rolling Hills and Golden Sands

34 top *The island of Corvo is the smallest of the western Azores. Vila Nova de Corvo, the tiny town seen in the picture (the island of Flores is visible in the distance), has no more than 400 permanent inhabitants.*

34 bottom *The territory commonly known as the Minho covers a larger area than that traced by the small, lush Rio Minho valley, in the extreme north of Portugal. In the valleys formed by the Lima, Cávado, Homem, and Tamega rivers the scenery alternates between terraced farmland (usually vineyards) and wild reliefs, with a sprinkling of chestnut trees.*

35 *The Minho offers extremely beautiful views. Plentiful in water, closed to the north by the mountains of Spanish Galicia and to the east by the serras of Trás-os-Montes, it is a region of extremes: dark sheets of water, pine and chestnut trees, small villages perched on the mountains or squashed at the bottom of the valley, and verdant scenery all around.*

The Minho:
the Green Heart
of Portugal

36 top and center *The whole Minho region, supplied by the intense rainfall typical of the oceanic climate of northern Portugal, abounds in water, which is collected in unusual artificial lakes called* barragems. *Small villages, prized crops, and wild vegetation sit on the shores of these basins.*

36 bottom *The rainfall is limited to eight months of the year and gives way to a period of relative dryness during the summer months. Thanks to this climate, the Minho valleys contain areas of intensive grapevine cultivation, which represents one of the region's few resources.*

36-37 *The Serra de Gerês is part of the Peneda-Gerês National Park, a magnificent nature reserve northeast of Braga, in the Minho. It is reached from Viana do Castelo, along the road that leads to the* barragems. *Natural and historic sights mingle in the heart of the park: the baroque palaces of Ponte de Lima, Romanesque bridges, paths in the forests, spectacular views of the surrounding mountains, and dams that supply the whole region with electricity.*

Looking out on the Atlantic

38 *Azenhas do Mar: the ocean heaves against the rocks, and perched dizzingly above the sea stand the fishermen's houses. One hundred sixty feet below, bathers splash in a hotel swimming pool. This too is Portugal: the work of man constantly contrasted with a gorgeous, untamed natural setting.*

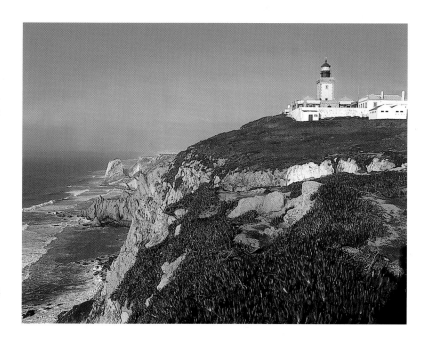

39 top *Beaten by strong winds all year round and situated approximately 460 feet above sea level, Cabo da Roca is the westernmost point of Portugal. It is wrongly believed to also be that of Europe, but the coasts of both Iceland and Ireland lie farther west.*

39 bottom *An extension of the Serra da Sintra, Cabo da Roca has, in the popular imagination, taken over from Cabo São Vicente, on the Algarve, long thought to be "the farthest edge of the world." The unceasing action of the ocean, shown here in all its might, has eroded the rock, creating a jagged coast full of delightfully secluded spots.*

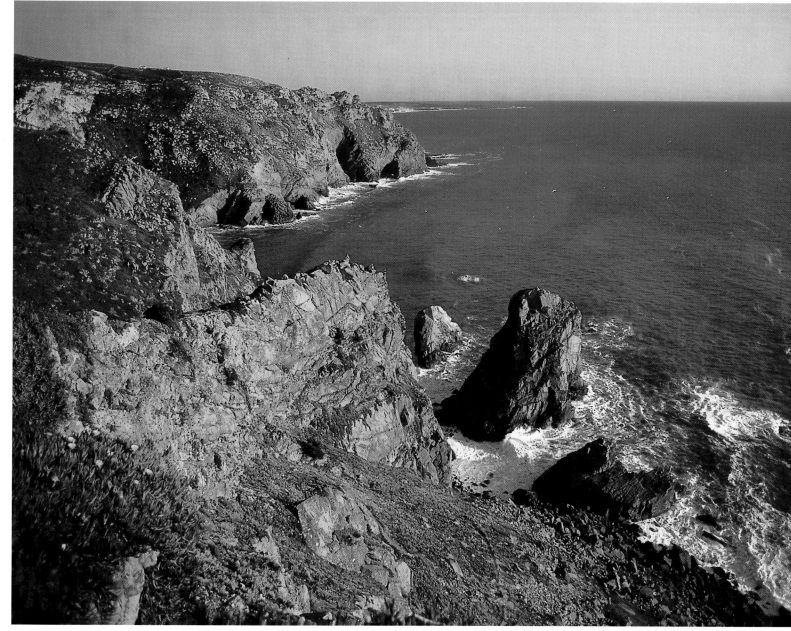

Wine-producing Country

40-41 *The Rio Douro valley (literally "river of gold") is one of the most fascinating regions in Portugal. Here they harvest some of the world's most famous grapes. The peasants have terraced the sides of the high ground and during the harvest men haul funnel-shaped baskets weighing more than 150 pounds. Two of the wines produced with these grapes are very famous:* vinho verde *takes its name from the color of the grapes and is a light wine;* vinho porto *is aged for anywhere between three and forty years and has a full-bodied flavor and a sturdy soul. The latter has been the object of commerce for more than three hundred years, since a peace treaty established free trading between England and Portugal. Legend has it that two English merchants invented port as it is known today by pouring spirit into the wine to stabilize it for transport. What is not legend is that some of the largest cellars were founded by the English between the seventeenth and eighteenth centuries.*

Sun-drenched Coasts

42-43 *Some postcards of Nazaré still show the fishermen, berets on their heads, drawing the boats out of the water aided by a pair of oxen. This tradition survived until just a few years ago on what many, quite rightly, consider the most authentic Portuguese coastline. The Algarve may be a gift of nature with its sea and tropical sands, but the Costa da Prata, especially in the immediate vicinity of Nazaré, is the Portugal of the ocean, rich and poor at the same time, charming and*

untamed despite the passing years and a never-ending stream of tourists. The Nazaré beach has been immortalized by generations of painters and photographers: fishermen busy mending nets, brightly-decorated boats drawn up on the beach fish left to dry in the sun, the sometimes violent sometimes gentle waves of the Atlantic, and small houses huddled together on the coast.
In summer, when the weather is good, it looks like the Mediterranean and is popular with surfers and wind-surfers. In winter, or in bad weather, the sea becomes master, eating up wide strips of sand and hiding the houses in thick fog. The village of Sitio peeks out from the top of a large rocky spur that shelters the village, protecting the beach from the strong winds that otherwise lash the coast.

44-45 *Many inhabitants of Lisbon still dream about having a home in Cascais. This picturesque little town has been a well-known resort since after the Second World War. Part of its success lies in its proximity (12 miles on the highway) to Lisbon for which it is little more than a suburb, or rather the capital's beach. Here the loveliest and most luxurious private villas are located. Some extend towards the great cliff that falls sheer into the sea; others (such as Villa Italia, for 37 years home to the exiled Savoy royal family) are hidden amid the vegetation, on the edge of the town. The old Cascais, a delightful seafaring village a stone's throw from Cabo da Roca, at the westernmost point on mainland Europe, is no more. In its place is a busy seaside resort, with plenty of* movida *and money. The most outstanding artistic and historical treasures that have survived the changes of the last 20 years are the* azulejos, *still to be seen in the ancient town hall and in the church of Nossa Senhora da Assunção.*

Alentejo: The Granary of the Country

46 left Monsarez is an ancient village-fortress on the border between the Alentejo and Spain that has maintained the original traits of the medieval village.

46 right Estremoz stands in the middle of that vast semi-flat region called Alentejo, situated east of Lisbon. It owes its fortune to the historical azulejo factory and the presence of one of the numerous royal country residences, now converted into a pousada (guesthouse).

46-47 The Alentejo is patronized by high-class, sentimental, and nostalgic tourists. The Braganzas spent much time here and this is where some of the most resolute democratic movements originated. The most attractive local residences have been turned into pousadas to accommodate this "sentimental" tourism.

48-49 The Alentejo is the heart of the older, rural Portugal. The landscape is that observed by the Portuguese kings from their "country" residences: cultivated fields, cork oaks, sheep, bulls, and the occasional village.

50-51 Monsanto, a picturesque village in Beira, was declared "the most characteristic village in Portugal" in the Fifties of the last century. The granite dwellings, flower-lined streets, and the fresh Manueline decorations won it a silver cockerel award, which is still perched on the church belltower.

The Algarve: the Garden of the West

52 top *Long considered the edge of the world, Cabo São Vicente is the westernmost tip of the Algarve.*

52 bottom *The extraordinary morphology of the Algarve (from the Arabic al-Gharb, "garden of the west") offers fantastic views. In some parts (as seen in the photograph at Sagres), the coast is cut into cliffs forming small inlets with delightful beaches; farther east, the coast is flat with huge beaches and coastal lagoons backed by great dunes.*

53 top *Midway between Portimão and Lagos, Praia da Rocha is one of the most famous spots on the Algarve. In the early twentieth century, Praia da Rocha was already renowned for its fine sandy beaches, encircled by erratically-shaped rocks eroded by the sea, and for its crystal-clear waters.*

53 bottom *The coast of Portimão, a well-known tourist resort in the heart of the Algarve, affords splendid views and is a paradise for old sea dogs. The sheer rocks form small bays in which to anchor, sheltered from the winds. Portimão has a memorable marine tradition; it is the most important port in the region and its inhabitants still make a living from tourism and sardine fishing.*

54-55 *White houses protruding towards the sea, the characteristic colored boats of the fishermen, and a clear blue sky all year round: the village of Ferragudo is all the beauty of the Algarve in a nutshell.*

56-57 *Color is a fundamental component on the Portuguese landscape. White walls and blue decorations are reminiscent of typically Mediterranean traditions. The red and green much used on boats are the favourite colors of the Portuguese people and appear on the national flag. For this house at Vila di Bispo on the Algarve, the traditional colors have been inverted: deep blue (with a touch of red) on the outside walls with white stucco-work and shutters.*

57 top and center *Vila do Bispo is a pretty seaside village situated six miles north of Sagres. Despite the tourist boom of recent years, the village has conserved its original appearance with small, blue and white houses, narrow streets, azulejos, and potted ficus trees for decoration.*

57 bottom *Tavira is a small town on the Algarve a few miles from Spain. It is famous for its Ancient Roman bridge over the Rio Asséca, for the Moorish castle that dominates the town, and for its past importance as a port. During its long history, the life of Tavira has always been inseparably bound to the sea and this is manifest in the decorations embellishing the churches. Both inside and out, as the picture shows, there is a prevalence of marine motifs (shells, stylized figure-heads, waves, and sea horses).*

58-59 *The most impressive rock of the Algarve (more than 500 feet high) rises from the sea near Vila do Bispo. All along the coast small, golden beaches give way to rocky stretches, eroded for centuries by the sea to form underground passages that fill with roaring waves.*

Madeira and the Azores: The Islands of Flowers

60-61 *The port of Velas is the largest town of São Jorge, in the Azores. Lying in the heart of the archipelago, the island is largely mountainous (with one peak rising to 3,494 feet) and rich in lush vegetation.*

61 left *A photograph taken beneath the Flamengos Mill is a must for tourists passing through Fayal, one of the smallest islands of the archipelago of the Azores. The island was named after the Myrica faya tree commonly found on the island.*

61 top right *For its size and beauty, São Miguel is the most famous of the Azores. It is of volcanic origin as clearly seen in this picture of one of the island's lagoons, formed by thousands of years of eruptions.*

61 bottom right *Teeming with flowers and not at all wild, despite having maintained its original appearance, blessed by a mild climate all year round and steady winds, the Azores are a paradise for sailing and deep-sea fishing enthusiasts. Together with Fayas, Pico (in the photograph) houses the Museu dos Baleeiros, dedicated to marine traditions and filled with exhibits relating to the whale-hunting practiced here in ancient times. Pico owes its name to the mountain that dominates the landscape, an extinct volcano and, at 7,609 feet, the highest peak in the Azores.*

62 top *Angra – its full name is Angra do Heroismo – is the only town on Terceira and the most important town in the Azores. An intact example of a Renaissance village, it has been declared a world heritage site by UNESCO.*

62 center *The island of Terceira was, for centuries, an obligatory stop for ships about to sail round Africa and head for India. All the major expeditions of the great Portuguese navigators, from Diaz to Da Gama stopped here for supplies or to shelter from storms. The highest point on the island and long a landmark for navigators is the Caldera de Santa Barbara.*

62 bottom *Terceira is famous the world over for its bullfights which differ from those of both Spain (bloodier) and those of Portugal (highly ritual and less bloody). As the name* tourada da corda *suggests, the bull is dragged through the streets tied to a rope. Naturally, the bull frees itself quite easily from this inadequate "leash" and runs free through the crowd, provoked by the most valiant who try to regain control.*

62-63 *Although it is the local craftsmanship – objects made by working fig tree pith or fish scales – that has made it famous all over the world, Flores, the most westerly of the Azores, boasts a natural beauty that makes it unique. It has an extremely uneven terrain, waterfalls, numerous volcanic lakes, and thick vegetation dominated by brightly-colored fragrant tropical flowers.*

64 top *At Câmara de Lobos, one of the towns on Madeira, they have for centuries fished black scabbard fish, one of the island's traditional dishes. The coastal scenery, gentle and bright, was immortalized in famous pictures painted by Winston Churchill, a frequent visitor to these parts.*

64 bottom *Funchal is the capital of Madeira. Despite conserving important traces of its past, the town now has modern buildings and good tourist facilities.*

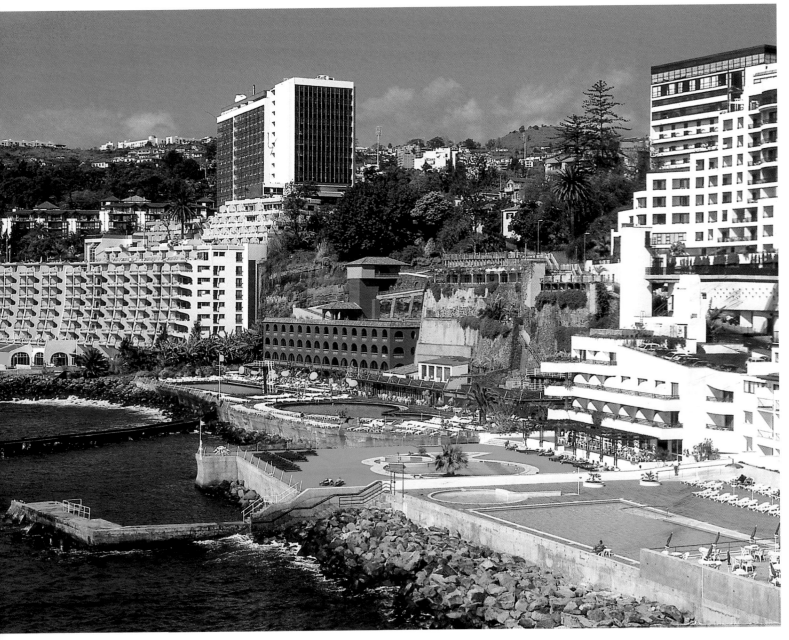

65 top *Much of the mountainous territory of Madeira has been turned into terraces, used to cultivate the grapes that produce the famous liqueur-like wine bearing the island's name. Madeira does not export wine alone: it is also famous for lace, wicker objects, and tropical flowers and fruit.*

65 bottom *Around Pico Ruivo and Paul da Serra, the mountainous area inland of Madeira returns to its original appearance. The earliest visitors to the island were greeted by a thick forest and called it Madeira, "wood" in Portuguese.*

66-67 *The coast of Porto Moniz, the second largest town on Madeira, is exposed to the winds and tides of the north, and is jagged and full of inlets. Nature seems to have delighted in creating striking views: sheer mountains rise above the sea and rivers of petrified lava, eroded by the sea, form the so-called "pools," natural basins that hold and heat the sea water.*

The Atmosphere
of the Metropolises

The castle of São Jorge offers great views of the Baixa, or lower town, the district of Lisbon razed to the ground by an earthquake in 1755 and reconstructed in just under 30 years in the French style in vogue at the time. Wide thoroughfares, impressive palaces, with characteristic amaranth-colored roofs replaced what remained of the old Moorish district, that worst hit by the catastrophe.

68 bottom *The Aqueduto das Aguas Livres crosses the entire Alcantara valley, on the edge of the Portuguese capital. It took more than three centuries to construct and definitively resolved Lisbon's recurrent problem: water shortage.*

69 *The monastery of Batalha combines the giddily spectacular Gothic with the sublime abundance of "chaotic" Manueline, a style custom-made for Portugal's golden era. The towers, spires, and ogival vaults of the monastery symbolize earthly aspirations to rise to the heavens, while shells, nets and hawsers recall the adventurous, oceanic dimensions of man's great exploits.*

Lisbon: The Nostalgic Capital

70-71 *There are many definitions for the Portuguese capital, and each is true: Lisbon is a city of a thousand faces, provincial and international, rich and poor. The signs of its grandeur are seen in the beauty of the Baixa (center), in the friezes adorning the Arch of Triumph (top left), the military museum (top right), or the entrance to the railway station (bottom right), and in the Padrão dos Descobrimentos (bottom left), the monument that more than any other celebrates the golden era and the country's desire to relaunch itself.*

72-73 *Praça do Comercio certainly has a spectacular appearance but the origins of this vast space were dramatic because the old royal palace, located on this site, was destroyed by an earthquake in 1755. In the background, the Arco Triunfal de Rua Augusta, and in front, an equestrian statue of José I. The Baixa begins beyond its arch.*

73 top *The 25 de Abril Bridge dominates the view to the west of Lisbon. More than a mile in length, it is the largest suspension bridge in Europe.*

73 center *Created in the first decades of this century, the Parque Eduardo VII takes its name from the British king who visited Lisbon in 1903. It is the largest park in the city.*

73 bottom *Like Belém, Alfama also survived the earthquake and thus conserves many traits of the Arab district of the past. Inhabited since the Middle Ages by fishermen, craftsmen, and small merchants, it later became the district of sailors and prostitutes. Today, rid of disease and filth, it is a living testimony to the appearance of the poorer parts of Lisbon.*

74-75 *The history of azulejos, decorative tiles that have over the years become the most original form of Portuguese art, is told in the Convento da Madre de Deus, since the 1800s the home of the Museu Nacional do Azulejo. The museum records the evolution of azulejos, from the early Arab pieces of the sixteenth century to the later Flemish-worked tiles. The art of the azulejos grew so rapidly that in the seventeenth century the fashion of* tapetes *(seen in blue in the photograph) emerged, with entire walls being tiled. The following century, it became customary practice to clad every valuable surface (churches, fountains, stairs) with the colored tiles.*

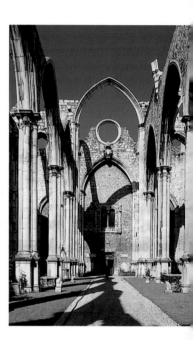

75 left and bottom right *Two views of the church (left) and chapter-house (bottom) of the Convento de Madre de Deus show the artistic wealth of the Manueline style, here combined with precious materials such as marble and wood from overseas colonies, and pure gold.*

75 top right *Built in the late fourteenth century, the Igreja do Carmo is a monument to the disaster that changed the history of Portugal, the earthquake. It collapsed on All Saints Day in 1755 and was intentionally not rebuilt as a tribute to the horror of that tragic day. It houses the Museu Arqueologico and, during good weather, open-air concerts.*

76 top *The Palácio Nacional de Ajuda was to replace the royal castle destroyed by the earthquake of 1755, but construction problems delayed its completion by more than a century. The finished monumental complex is smaller than originally intended and the façade has the clearly neo-classical appearance typical of Romanticism.*

76 center *Along with the Teatro Nacional Dona Maria II, the Teatro São Carlos is where the opera and ballet lovers of the Portuguese capital meet. Spectacular, majestic, and blessed with uncommon acoustic qualities, this theater offers the best of the European program to Portuguese enthusiasts. The theater, opera, and, more generally, artistic seasons are busy and much appreciated in a city with illustrious traditions that sees the promotion of culture as a policy for advancement.*

76 bottom *Opened in 1962 in the Palácio Pimenta, the Museu da Cidade provides visitors with a historical perspective of the history of Lisbon. Of particular interest, the room dedicated to the earthquake contains a model of the city as it was before that fateful day in 1755.*

76-77 The interior of the elegant and opulent Palácio Nacional de Ajuda shows signs of the royal family's passage. The building was, however, inhabited by the monarchs for just 50 years, between 1861 and 1910. After that date, the apartments were opened to the public. Besides precious furnishings and tapestries, it contains 20 marble statues made in the late nineteenth century by sculptors of the Mafra school.

78 top *Among the countless museums of Lisbon, the Museu Nacional dos Coches (carriage museum) always arouses much curiosity. Created at the wishes of the Portuguese royal family in the early 1900s, the museum offers the most spectacular collection of ancient coaches and vintage cars in Europe.*

78 center *Housed in a west wing of the Mosteiro dos Jerónimos, the Museu da Marinha was founded in 1863. Its major attractions include numerous models of fishing vessels and warships, original nautical charts, and the Santa Clara seaplane, the first plane to fly across the Atlantic, on the Lisbon-Rio de Janeiro route. Impressive statues are dedicated to the leading figures in Portuguese maritime history. The most important of course is the "father" of the colonial adventure, Henry the Navigator (at the center of the picture), who founded the school of navigation at Sagres.*

78 bottom *In additionto a rich collection of azulejos and panels portraying some of the major battles in Portuguese history, the Museu Militar – seen here is a room of clearly pompous baroque inspiration – possesses a rich collection of Portuguese, French, English, Spanish, Dutch, and Arab firearms.*

79 *The Museu da Marinha exhibits numerous works dedicated to the kings and navigators that marked the history of Portugal. The pictures show two noblemen who governed the overseas provinces: João de Castro (left) and Francisco de Almedia (right), governor of India in the early 1500s.*

80 top *Details of the cloister of the Mosteiro dos Jerónimos reveal distinctive Manueline traits: complex ornamentation of pillars and vaults, bas-reliefs covering the columns, an evident mixture of styles, and the double two-light arches with typically oriental decorations.*

80 bottom *The Mosteiro dos Jerónimos is probably the most famous monument in Lisbon. Having survived the eighteenth-century earthquake, it shows to its fullest the style that marked Portugal's golden era, that of King Manuel I. The church of Santa Maria, in the center of the monastery, is a summary of this art and, in a broad sense, of Portuguese history too. It is a blend of the most diverse forms and with varied contributions, a tribute to the cosmopolitanism of the Manueline empire. Symbols of seafaring exploits are mixed with the customary signs of Catholic devotion, Arab decorations (clearly visible in this picture of the vault) mix with ones typically Western.*

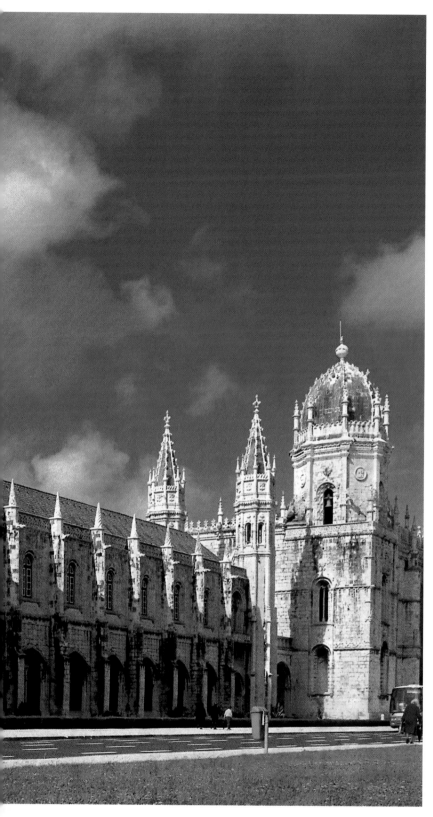

81 top *With his naval adventures, Vasco da Gama, the great navigator and symbol of the golden era, earned himself eternal rest within the walls of the Mosteiro dos Jerónimos. His tomb is visited by thousands of people every year.*

81 bottom *This picture taken from the River Tagus shows a charming view of the Praça do Imperio gardens, with the Fonte Luminosa and the splendid Mosteiro dos Jerónimos, perhaps the most beautiful monument in Lisbon.*

80-81 The magnificent Mosteiro dos Jerónimos was made in pure Manueline style. Originally, the huge monastery of the Hieronymites stood on the banks of the Tagus. However, construction of the dock diverted the course of the river and led to the birth of the Praça do Imperio and the Avenida da India.

Queluz: The Portuguese Versailles

82 *The small village of Queluz (literally "what light!"), on the outskirts of Lisbon, boasts the summer residence of the royal Braganza family. Considered the "Portuguese Versailles," the Palácio Nacional de Queluz dates from the end of the eighteenth century and is now a splendid example of rococo, albeit mixed in some parts with neo-classical elements. The project was completed by two great eighteenth-century architects: Mateus Vicente de Oliveira and Jean-Baptiste Robillon.*

82-83 *The interiors of the Palácio Nacional de Queluz are sumptuous, as a royal residence should be. Of all the rooms, lit by enormous crystal chandeliers and decorated with inlaid furniture and fine marble, the Sala do Trono gives a special thrill. A triumph of stucco-work and gilt, thanks to its size and acoustics it serves as an auditorium during the Sintra Music Festival.*

Porto:
Work is
the Creed

84-85 *Praça da Libertade is the heart of Porto, the capital of the north. An industrious and thriving city, its present prosperity comes from the service sector and, at least in part, from sea trade. Elegant in the center, chaotic on the outskirts, the city conserves the layout of a coastal city, descending from the vineyards of Gondomar towards the port of Leixões.*

85 top *The modern and well-equipped port of Leixões is Porto's window on the world. The city is the second largest in Portugal with more than 1,500,000 inhabitants in the metropolitan area and has maintained its traditional "privileged" trading relations with Latin America, England, and France.*

85 center *The Ribeira is the oldest district in Porto, the only true urban legacy of the old port-city. The streets are narrow and filled with small shops, the houses higher and deeper than they are wide with a minimal façade; the lower classes live here, just a stone's throw from the symbol of the city's wealth, the Stock Exchange.*

85 bottom *The famous barcos rebelos are still a common sight along the docks and under the Dom Luis iron bridge. These are traditional vessels used for centuries, until recent decades, to transport casks of wine down the Rio Douro, from the* quintas *where it is produced and aged, to the wharves of Porto where it is loaded on merchant ships that set sail for all parts of the world.*

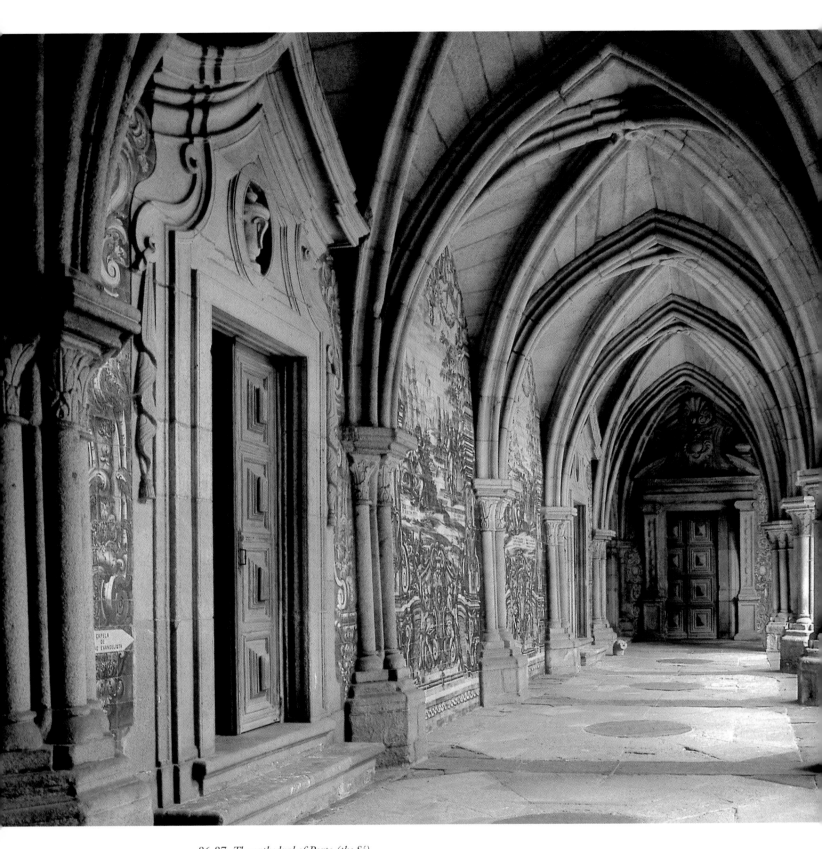

86-87 *The cathedral of Porto (the Sé),
built in the twelfth century in
Romanesque style, has been repeatedly
tampered with but conserves the stern
appearance of religious buildings
constructed in that period, more fortresses
than churches. Along the walls of the
cloister (in the picture), eighteenth-
century* tapetes *depict the "Song of
Songs" and the "Metamorphoses."*

87 top The tapetes, *traditional art that flourished during the so-called "golden age," have continued to clad the walls of public building right through to the modern era. The monumental but "cold" hall of the railway station of São Bento in Porto was embellished in 1916 with numerous* azulejos *portraying scenes of everyday Portuguese life from past centuries.*

87 bottom *The Sé of Porto, originally conceived as a fortified church hence its rather austere appearance, owes part of its present-day charm to its* azulejos. *From numerous details it is possible to notice the type and number of decorative additions made over the centuries in the most diverse styles to the original Romanesque style of the church. Many parts of the cathedral were built when Manueline style was at its peak, as is shown by this column in the square in front of the basilica.*

Braga:
The Town
of Prayer

88-89 *An unusual double flight of baroque steps ascends the hill dominated by the sanctuary of Bom Jesus do Monte, situated in the middle of a splendid park much-loved by the people of Braga.*

89 top *Braga is a dynamic and modern city that has not forgotten its past. Full churches and sanctuaries are an indication of the "religious" inclinations of this town set in the heart of the Minho. At the same time, the elegant, newly-restored buildings and well-tended baroque gardens show instead that the money of the economic boom of recent years has been well spent.*

89 center *Praça da República is the urban and social heart of Braga where the city* movida *enlivens the porticoes and paved square. This is a relatively recent phenomenon, since at the beginning of this century the famous Spanish writer Miguel de Unamuno, when a guest here, complained that the streets of the pious Braga were deserted from dusk to dawn.*

89 bottom *Perhaps for its strategic position (the five most important roads in Portugal passed through Bragara Augusta, as it was called), perhaps because it was the seat of an archbishopric as early as the twelfth century, Braga became a sort of Portuguese Rome. The powerful local clergy left behind a splendid artistic heritage, from numerous monasteries to an interminable string of churches and chapels.*

Sintra: A Pearl Set in the Woods

90 top left *Sintra boasts the most unusual castle in the land, the Palácio da Pena: a unique ensemble of domes, drawbridges, minarets, and towers in various mixed styles – along the lines of the Bavarian castles – set atop the highest mountain in the area.*

90 center left *A few miles from the Palácio Nacional da Pena, the Quinta de Monserrate, a nineteenth-century villa in Moorish style, stands in English gardens filled with subtropical plants and tree-ferns.*

90 bottom left *Wilhelm von Eschwege, a nineteenth-century German aristocrat, was commissioned to build "the most romantic palace in the world," combining all styles in a single construction. The result was the Palácio da Pena, of which a frieze is shown here.*

90 center right *The architect who designed the Palácio Nacional da Pena used decorative elements typical of to Lisbon: the picture shows the diamond-pointed rustication originally used for the Casa dos Bicos, applied here to the wall of one of the entrance portals.*

90-91 *The Palácio Nacional da Pena, set in a fairy-tale park on the Serra da Sintra, was for many years the summer residence of the royal family. Only the flight of the Braganza family brought the monarchical history of Portugal and the castle to a close.*

92 top *Nearly 1,640 feet high, looming above Sintra, the Castelo dos Mouros was built between the eighth and ninth centuries. Of the original construction only the battlements and towers have survived.*

92 bottom *A visit to the Palácio Nacional reveals several pleasant surprises. The furnishings, the wooden, marble, or azulejos paneling (present in nearly all the rooms), the precious floors, and the very history intrinsic to its every part blend to create an extraordinary atmosphere.*

93 top *The Palácio Nacional (known as Paço Real to avoid confusion with the Palácio Nacional da Pena) dominates the skyline of Sintra, a lovely town immersed in the fascinating, wooded Serra of the same name. The main body of the building was erected in the fifteenth century, and the two huge, conical chimneys that used to be part of the royal kitchen, added in the seventeenth century, can be seen from afar.*

93 bottom *The Sala dos Brasoes (or blazons, also known as the Stag Room) is one of the most impressive rooms in the Palácio Nacional of Sintra. The ceiling is an octagonal wooden dome, painted in the early 1500s; prancing stags support the coats of arms of the noble Portuguese families. In the middle of the dome is the blazon of Manuel I. The walls of the room are lined with* azulejos *depicting hunting scenes.*

Inland Treasures

94 top right *Tomar, built in the Nabao Valley, in the heart of Estremadura, is the city of the Templars. The whole town is dominated by the great convent-castle of the Knights Templar, surrounded by a forest of pine trees and the home of two orders (Templars and Order of Christ).*

94 top left *Declared a national monument, Obidos is one of the pearls of the Costa da Prata. Entirely fortified, it is also delicately beautiful in parts.*

94 bottom left *The fortifications (the picture shows the castle built in 1171 by the Templars at Amoural, at the confluence of the Tagus and the Rio Zêzere) erected over the centuries all over Portugal bear witness to a troubled history plagued by war. After the fall of the Roman empire, the country was first invaded by the Visigoths and then the Moors. The oldest Portuguese castles, built at strategic points in the mountainous regions and the Asturias, date from that time and from the centuries of the reconquest. The Castilian-style constructions date from the late-Middle Ages, when at the cost of long and ferocious wars, the Portuguese won independence from Spain.*

95 *Like many of the constructions of the period (twelfth century), the Sé Velha, the old cathedral of Coimbra, resembles a fortress more than a church. Only the Porta Especiosa and the belfry adorned with Renaissance motifs differ from the somber style of the rest of the building.*

96-97 *The famous Wine Route, the memorable road along the Rio Douro has one obligatory stop: the Solar de Mateus. A baroque mansion built in the eighteenth century at Vila Real by the counts of Mateus, the solar is the emblem of a wine empire famous throughout the world. The wine made with the grapes of this region is called Mateus and carries the distinctive façade of the owner's villa on the label.*

Guimarães: The Cradle of the Braganza Family

98-99 *The cloister of the Museu Alberto Sampaio in Guimarães consists of a beautiful loggia and a secluded courtyard with French garden flaunting the characteristic Manueline ornamental motifs. The museum is one of the most important in Portugal and houses the treasure of the Dukes of Braganza – precious silver objects and a portable altar decorated in bas-relief.*

99 left *The chapel of the Palace of the Dukes of Braganza is a fine example of Gothic with just a few Manueline additions. The picture also shows the high, pointed stained glass windows that illuminate the two wooden women's galleries.*

99 right *The Palace of the Dukes of Braganza (top, with its characteristic chimneys) and the castle (bottom, seen here are the towers, walls, and entrance) share a somber and essential style and are the two most impressive buildings of Guimarães, the home of the Braganza family.*

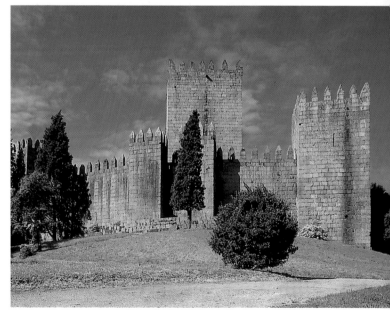

"Buen retiro" of the Mascarenhas

100 top *Situated on the edge of the Parque Florestal de Monsanto on the outskirts of Lisbon, the Palácio dos Marques de Fronteira was built for Dom João Mascarenhas in Italian Renaissance style. Members of the noble family still live here and stroll through its extensive and gorgeous gardens. Some of the rooms in the palace and the gardens, famous for the decorative plant sculptures, splendid* azulejos, *and the numerous neo-classical works, are open to visitors accompanied by a guide.*

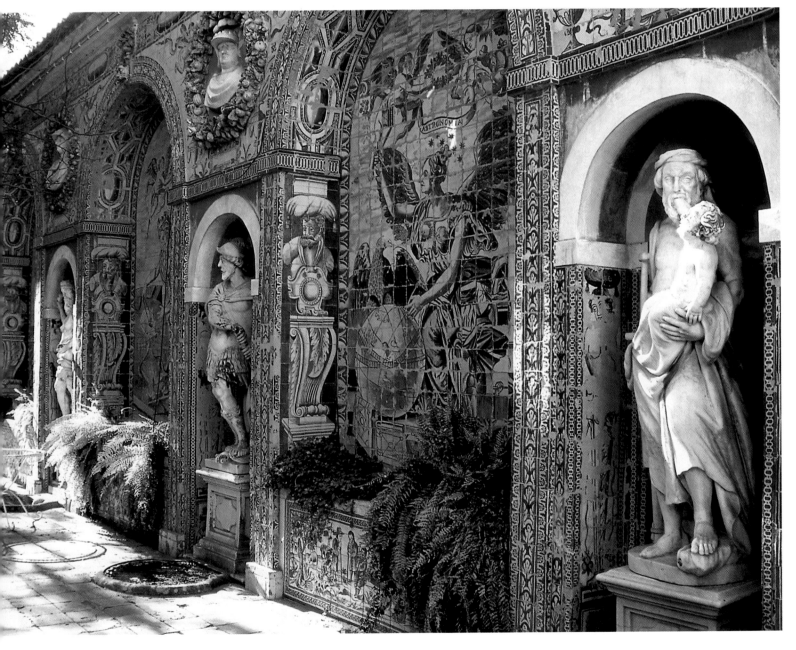

100 bottom *The Palácio dos Marques de Fronteira is renowned more for its beautiful gardens than for the design of the building. The garden of Venus and the Italian garden, designed in the seventeenth century, are particularly attractive. A visit to the park is like taking a stroll through an open-air museum: paths, grottoes, and terraces are lined with* azulejos *painted by the masters of the seventeenth century and small niches house busts of sovereigns and reproductions of classical statues.*

101 *The treasure of the gardens of Palácio dos Marques de Fronteira is the Kings' Gallery, a row of knights all portrayed on blue and white* tapetes of azulejos. *Two staircases rise around the Moorish-style pool allowing the masterpiece to be admired from several angles. The majolicas that adorn the gardens, especially those in the Kings' Gallery, are considered the highest expression of this art: the refined motifs were painted for the first time in two colors on glazed tiles.*

Batalha: Stone Tracery

102 Along with the Mosteiro dos Jerónimos of Lisbon, the monastery of Santa Maria da Vitoria in Batalha is unanimously considered a masterpiece of Manueline art. Built at the end of the fourteenth century in Gothic style – of which clear traces remain in the façade (top right) and in the ogival arches of the interior (left) – mixed with Renaissance elements, it was completed after two centuries in keeping with the style in vogue at the time, thus meeting the highest Manueline standards. The mixture of styles has produced effects of remarkable beauty, as in the case of the Capela do Fundador (bottom right) with its pointed Gothic arches closed by a splendid star vault of Manueline inspiration.

103 The Claustro Real is the heart of the monastery of Santa Maria da Vitoria. Like the building's main body, it was designed it was designed in Gothic style, but tampered with during the golden era. To instil in those observing it a sense of Portugal's new colonial wealth, the ogival windows were given stone gratings, defined by some as "embroidered stone."

In the Footsteps of Caesar

104-105 and 105 right *Valuable evidence of the passage of the Romans has been found in archaeological sites on the* planicies *(plains),the region between the Tagus River and the Spanish border. Nearly all traces of the Roman era came to the light as a result of the 1755 earthquake, so violent that it literally lifted the lid off the places now excavated. The Roman temple of Evora, a town on the* planicies *particularly prosperous in imperial times, is one of the most famous and interesting monuments to have survived the passing centuries and repeated interventions from the Middle Ages on. A Corinthian-style peripteral temple, dedicated either to Diana or more probably the worship of the emperor, is one of the best preserved on the peninsula. Built in the town acropolis in the second century B.C., it was turned into a fortress in mediaeval times and then restored to much of its former splendor in the late nineteenth century.*

105 left *In 137 B.C. Lisbon and the rest of Portugal at last became part of the expanding Roman empire. After overcoming the local Iberian and Celtic peoples as well as, above all, the Carthaginians, the Roman legions advanced from north to south, leaving traces of their passage everywhere, both outside the settlements, as shown by finds made all over the* planicies *(plains), and in the towns, which progressively incorporated the imperial remains. Excellent examples of this are two monuments in Evora: the Roman or Dona Isabel Gate (top), partially modified in subsequent eras, and the Rectangular Tower (bottom) a mediaeval construction on a Roman base.*

A Thousand Faces,
a Hundred Races, One Soul

106 top *When the students of the famous university of Coimbra celebrate the end of the school year in May, they hold the Queima da Fitas, during which fresh graduates burn the symbols of the faculty after a lively procession. They then party until dawn to the sound of the* fado.

106 bottom *In Portugal, culture is not confined to museums or school. The Portuguese take pride in their being and appreciate all art forms that bring out their "essence." In Lisbon, this diverges slightly with the capital's legitimate aspirations to be a European metropolis in the cultural sense. The result is a varied and lively cultural framework with exhibitions, theater and opera seasons, as well as ballet or folk dancing every month of the year.*

107 *Coimbra, the capital of Portugal from the twelfth to the thirteenth century, is today a busy town with 150,000 inhabitants (435,000 in the metropolitan area). It owes its revival to the university, which moved here from Lisbon at the beginning of the fourteenth century. The institution bestows both human and financial resources at all levels to the city. Coimbras liveliness is not only economic or intellectual but (as seen in the photo depicting a scene from the Queimada Fitas) also* movida, *the desire to live it up and have fun inthe most free and easy ways.*

The Call of the Ocean

108 *Life in Portugal has always been lived on the sea shores. The inland areas may have guaranteed refuge and food during invasions, but the country's true wealth is the ocean. Sailed by* moliceiros *and large fishing boats, whalers and merchant ships, caravels and galleons, the Atlantic made Portugal a nation, as all the aspirations and hopes of the Portuguese people were placed in that great imperial adventure of colonialism.*

109 *Unmistakable in shape and color, for years the* moliceiros *bore generations of fishermen along the coasts of Portugal. Today they are also a source of tourist income. The attractions of the Atlantic beaches now include these unusual boats hand-painted in bright colors by the fishermen themselves or, in some cases, by artist-craftsmen now specialized in the creation of new designs, mostly for the benefit of visitors. This minimal tourist exploitation of a traditional art should not be judged harshly: the recent "re-elaborations" are fruit of the same culture that produced the originals, which – it must be stressed – still sail the Portuguese waters. A common feature of all the* moliceiros *is the curved or square high bow: this usually bears the most beautiful decorations, forming a sort of gaudy figure-head featuring attractive women and marine motifs.*

110 and 111 *The produce of the sea is still one of Portugal's greatest assets. The whalers and transoceanic fishing expeditions are no more, but mackerel, sardines, and shellfish still fully meet the domestic demand and are exported to and appreciated all over Europe. The fishing fleet partially supplies of Portuguese industry but, above all, fills the local restaurants with huge quantities of fresh produce. As a result, many Portuguese recipes feature fish dishes. In Lisbon as at*

Nazaré (where sardines are still dried in the sun at the water's edge), in Porto and on the Algarve, fish reign supreme: caldeirada (fish soup), sole, turbot, white bream, mullet, as well as grilled swordfish and hake are common. Another star of the Portuguese table is bacalhau, or cod, (there are said to be 365 ways of cooking it, one for every day of the year), usually assado, fried, or cozido, boiled and served with potatoes and a little olive oil. A must with every fish dish is of course a bottle of vinho verde *produced in the Minho region or in the Douro Valley.*

112-113 and 113 *Obliged by continental tradition to perform humble tasks in the fields, the ox has been redeemed on the Portuguese coasts. Having abandoned the fatigue of the plough, oxen in pairs aid the fishermen in their work. In particular, they serve as a power source in drawing the boats a shore after a fishing trip. Technological progress has come also to this edge of mainland Europe, which,*

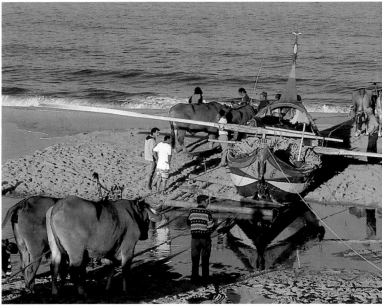

although reluctant to embrace the boldest innovations, has nearly everywhere adopted internal combustion engines and jiggers. It is still possible, however, on some beaches of the Costa da Prata – at Aveiro (in the pictures) and at Nazaré – to admire the oxen at their ancient toil on the shore, proof that, despite change, Portugal is still a humble country bound to tradition.

Feiras and Folklore

114 and 114-115 *In Portugal, it is not unusual i to happen upon a fair or a festival, especially between May and October. As in many Latin countries, Portugal conserves great religious traditions, most mixed somewhat with local semi-pagan rituals that blend the stories of the saints with lay folklore and legend. The most famous festivals include the Dos Santos Populares in Lisbon (June), Nossa Senhora dos Navigantes at Cascais (Assumption Day), the Holy Trinity in Batalha (mid-June), the Queima das Fitas in Coimbra (May), the Romaria de Nossa Senhora da Nazaré (September) the Dos Tabuleiros celebrations at Tomar (Whit Sunday), São Joao at Porto (June 22nd/23rd), and Nossa Senhora da Agonia at Viana do Castelo (August). For each of these feiras out come the traditional costumes (red and white dresses with bodices, with lace and filigree jewelry for the women, and white shirts with waistcoats and berets or hard-brimmed black hats for the men) and all go off to dance to the rhythm of tambourines and guitars.*

116 and 116-117 *Portuguese music and dancing, much like the large majority of its literature, are little known outside the country. Yet the musical seasons, in Lisbon especially, are first class and generally well attended. A distinction must, however, be made between international and local music: the former is presented in the Teatro Nacional Opera House in Lisbon and at the Festival Internacional de Musica of Sintra; the latter is relegated to provincial festivals and a role of folk tradition in public places. This is not the case of* fado, *the Portuguese "Blues" played every evening in Coimbra, Porto, Braga, and in the capital. Whether in small restaurants where they serve freshly-caught fish or in the countless Fado Houses, the guitar accompanies the melancholic song that may have originated in Brazil, or perhaps in Africa, and that embodies the deepest expression of the Portuguese soul,* saudade *(a mixture of homesickness and emptiness).*

118 top right and left *The religious bond that unites all Portuguese does not slacken even with an ocean between them, as revealed by the festivals that animate the Azores several times a year, in which of all the inhabitants actively participate. During the festival of Sant'Anna at São Miguel, the congregation carry heavy wooden statues through the streets of Furnas (bottom). At Pico, for the Holy Spirit celebrations, the ancient custom of carrying bread in procession before blessing it lives on (top).*

118 bottom right *The greatest religious celebrations are those held in Braga, the cradle of Portuguese Catholicism. During Holy Week, the faithful walk in procession on both Holy Thursday and Good Friday along the walls of the old Roman town, stopping at the* passos, *small altars set up along the way.*

119 *The most famous festival of Viana do Castelo, along the Costa Verde, is that of Nossa Senhora da Agonia. The climax of the event is held on Saturday, when a hoard of people in costume flood the streets, accompanied by music and wine. Similar enthusiasm is aroused for the celebrations of the Cross, during which the procession takes the form of a parade, with great local participation.*

120-121 and 121 Touradas, *the Portuguese bullfights, are fascinating and spectacular but unlike those of Spain, not bloody. In otherwords, even if the bull is injured it is not slaughtered. Its horns are bound with padding to reduce the danger and limit the risks of injury to the bullfighters, who are not only on foot, as in Spain, but on* horseback too. The decision to make the touradas *less violent was made following a serious accident in which Count d'Arcos was killed. The king was deeply distressed by the death of his relative and so issued a series of precautions to reduce accidents. Since then, bulls and bullfighters have left the arena alive and, at the most, suffer* only the odd minor injury, cured in a few days. In contrast, the poetic vein of the *tourada has been accentuated with magnificent costumes, sometimes original eighteenth-century ones with wig and three-pointed hat, and symbolic gestures (such as the prentend killing of the bull with a flower instead of a sword).*

122-123 *Portuguese golf courses are just as efficient, prestigious, and technically valid as the best greens throughout Europe and the rest of the world. Particularly famous are those in the elegant suburbs of Porto and Lisbon and on the Algarve, very green and often situated spectacularly above the sea.*

121

Coimbra:
The Roots of a New Portugal

124 Coimbra, the first capital of Portugal, is now known as "the learned" for its crucial role in the country's cultural development. Here, Portugal realized its hopes of attaching itself to the European locomotive to revive its economy after two centuries of decline. These hopes were made tangible in 1986 when the country joined the European Union and in 1999 when Portugal adopted the single currency. Coimbra is waging its hopes of becoming the nation's third metropolis on its university. Of medieval origin, it is one of the most prestigious on the continent, as is shown by the buildings used to house the offices, lecture rooms, and, above all, the library, a baroque gem containing more than 30,000 books plus a section devoted to rare medieval manuscripts. The heart of the university is the Sala dos Capelos (top left) where the most important moments of the academic year are lived.

125 Founded in 1290, the University of Coimbra had to share onus and honor with Lisbon until 1537, when it was reformed by King João III and turned into an independent academy. Since then, it has constantly grown to become a leading European cultural pole. Although constant modernization has given the faculty and academic institutes cutting-edge facilities, Coimbra maintains certain age-old traditions that make it a "special" school. These range from the ceremonies at the beginning (in the picture) and end of the school year to formal graduations and the repúblicas.

126-127 The repúblicas are characteristic "hostels" run by the Coimbra University students themselves. Grouped in communities of 15 or 20, called repúblicas, they govern themselves in total freedom, sharing domestic duties, financial resources, and academic experiences.

128 The image shows the spire and statue of the Redeemer, towering above the sanctuary of Fátima.

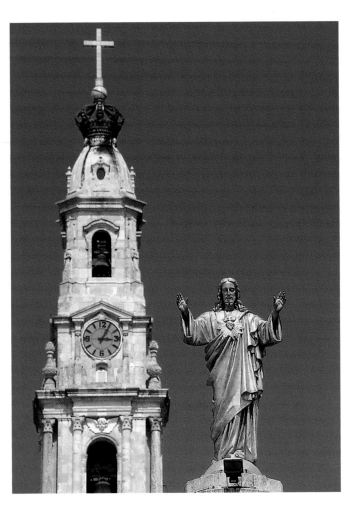

Illustration credits:

Stefano Amantini / Atlantide: pages 46-47.

Antonio Attini / Archivio White Star: pages 30-31, 68, 70 top, 70-71, 71, 73 top right, center and bottom, 75 top, 76 top, 76-77, 78, 79, 80, 81, 104 top, 104 center left, 104 bottom, 105, 106 bottom, 114-115, 116, 117.

B.A.E.Inc/Alamy: pages 32-33.

Bruno Barbier / Ag. Speranza: pages 114 top, 119, 121.

Bruno Barbier / Hémispheres: pages 12-13, 19, 40 bottom, 60-61, 89 bottom, 108, 114 bottom, 118 top, 120-121, 125.

Fausto Giaccone / Ag. Speranza: pages 106 top, 107, 118 bottom right, 124 bottom, 126-127.

Fausto Giaccone / SIE: pages 42 right, 114-115.

François Gohier / Ag. Speranza: page 63 bottom.

David W. Hamilton / Image Bank: page 45 bottom.

Franck Lechenet / Hémisperes: pages 14-15, 62 center.

Marco Leopardi / SIE: pages 48-49.

W. Louvet / Ag. Visa: pages 109 top, 112, 113.

Marco Mairani / Focus Team: page 45 top.

Jose Manuel / Image Bank: pages 22 bottom, 90 top.

Orbassano / Focus Team: pages 110 top left, 111 left.

Jean Charles Pinheira: pages 34 top, 38, 44-45, 61 top, 62 top, 62-63, 64 top, 70 bottom, 74-75, 75 bottom, 76 center and bottom, 85 bottom, 92 bottom, 93, 100, 101, 110 bottom, 118 bottom left.

Massimo Ripani/Sime/Sie: pages 72-73.

Stefano Scatà / Image Bank: page 65 bottom.

Schinco / Focus Team: page11.

Tavanti / Focus Team: pages 20-21, 65 top.

Angelo Tondini / Focus Team: pages 10 top left, 45 center.

Yvan Travert / Ag. Speranza: pages 39 bottom, 64 bottom, 66-67, 88-89, 96-97.

Giulio Veggi / Archivio White Star: pages 1, 2-3, 4-5, 6-7, 8, 9, 10 top right, 10 center, 10 bottom, 16-17, 18, 22 top, 23, 24-25, 27, 28-29, 29, 34 bottom, 35, 36, 37, 40 top, 40-41, 42 left, 42-43, 46, 50-51, 52, 53, 54-55, 56, 57, 58-59, 69, 82, 83, 84-85, 85 top and center, 86, 87, 89 top and center, 90 center right, 90 bottom, 92 top, 94, 95, 98, 99, 102, 103, 104 center right, 109 bottom, 110 top right, 122-123, 124 top, 128.

Pawel Wysocki / Hémispheres: pages 39 top, 90 center left, 90-91.

C. Alberto Zabert / Realy Easy Star: pages 62 bottom, 111 right.

128